P9-EJS-652

CH

EDGE BOOKS™

HALLOWEEN EXTREME

HOW TO CREATE

Spectacular HALLOWEEN Costumes

by Louann Brown and
Jason Nemeth

CAPSTONE PRESS
a capstone imprint

Edge Books are published by Capstone Press,
151 Good Counsel Drive, P.O. Box 669, Mankato, Minnesota 56002.
www.capstonepub.com

 Books published by Capstone Press are manufactured with paper
containing at least 10 percent post-consumer waste.

Library of Congress Cataloging-in-Publication Data
Brown, Louann Mattes.
How to Create Spectacular Halloween Costumes / by Louann Mattes Brown
and Jason Nemeth.
p. cm. — (Edge books. Halloween extreme)
Includes bibliographical references and index.
Summary: "Provides step-by-step instructions for making Halloween costumes
    using household materials"—Provided by publisher.
ISBN 978-1-4296-5422-7 (library binding)
1. Halloween costumes—Juvenile literature. I. Nemeth, Jason D. II. Title.
    III. Series.
TT633.B764 2011
646.4'78—dc22   2010030392

Editorial Credits
Megan Peterson and Shelly Lyons, editors; Tracy Davies, designer;
    Sarah Schuette, photo stylist; Marcy Morin, project production;
    Eric Manske, production specialist

Photo Credits
All photos by Capstone Studio/Karon Dubke

Artistic Credits
Shutterstock/AKaiser, Merkushev Vasiliy, Randall Mikulas, Renee Reeder
    BFA, Steven Bourelle

Printed in the United States of America in Stevens Point, Wisconsin.
052011   006210R

Table of Contents

Introduction

Did you ever wish you could change into a howling wolf or bloodsucking vampire? Halloween is the day your wicked dreams can come true. All it takes to create your one-of-a-kind costume is a little planning and a few materials. The extreme costumes in this book are sure to get you noticed while trick-or-treating.

If you want to create a truly eye-catching and inexpensive costume, be sure to plan ahead. Have an adult take you to yard sales and second-hand stores to look for used clothing. Buy accessories and face paints on sale after Halloween is over. Talk to the manager of a department store and ask for donations of cardboard. Save old cereal and pizza boxes. Work in an open space such as a basement, backyard, or garage. And be sure to ask an adult for help when using dangerous tools, such as a hot glue gun or utility scissors.

So what are you waiting for?
It's never too early to start creating
your spectacular Halloween costume!

Tools

glue gun and
hot glue

measuring tape

hole punch

utility scissors

Don't Feed the Sharks

You caught the big wave, but the shark caught you! Surf for candy in a costume that tells the tale. Be sure to warn your friends about the shark that's loose in the neighborhood.

WHAT YOU NEED:
marker
ruler
large piece of cardboard
utility scissors
spray paint
red acrylic paint
paintbrush
T-shirt
sunglasses
shorts
sandals

Step 1: Draw a 3- by 1-foot (0.9- by 0.3-meter) surfboard shape on a piece of cardboard. Cut it out with a utility scissors.

Step 2: Use spray paint to paint your surfboard. Follow the instructions and safety precautions on the can. Let dry.

Step 3: Draw a jagged half-circle on one side of the surfboard. Cut it out. Paint the jagged edge red to look like blood. Let dry.

Step 4: Use the utility scissors to shred the end of one of the T-shirt's sleeves. Paint the edges red. Let dry.

Step 5: Put on your sunglasses, T-shirt, shorts, and sandals. Tuck one arm inside your shirt on the side you shredded. Carry your surfboard with your other hand.

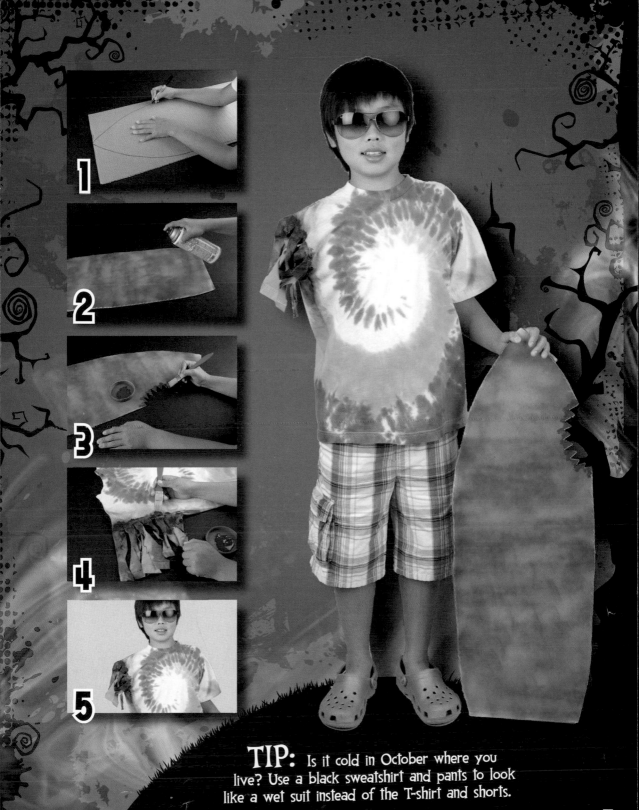

TIP: Is it cold in October where you live? Use a black sweatshirt and pants to look like a wet suit instead of the T-shirt and shorts.

Shadow of Death

Can a person escape the shadow of death? Amaze your friends with this terrific **illusion**. No matter how fast the person runs, death is right behind.

WHAT YOU NEED:

glue gun and hot glue
white, long-sleeved
    turtleneck
fabric scissors
ruler
2 pizza box lids
paintbrush
white acrylic paint
black marker
1- by 36-inch (2.5- by
    91-centimeter) strip
    of black cloth
measuring tape
old white bedsheet
white gloves
black hoodie
black pants
socks

Step 1: Ask an adult to help you hot glue the neck and cuffs of the white turtleneck closed. Set aside.

Step 2: Cut out a 7- by 9-inch (18- by 23-centimeter) pear-shaped head from a pizza box lid. Paint it white. Let dry.

Step 3: Turn the head so the wide end is at the top. Using a black marker, draw a long oval mouth, two small nostrils, large eyes, and raised eyebrows.

Step 4: Flip over the head so the blank side is showing. Ask an adult to help you hot glue each end of the black cloth to the top of the head. Hot glue the bottom of the head to the neck of the turtleneck. Let dry.

Step 5: Hang the cardboard head around your neck. Ask an adult to measure from the bottom of the shirt to the cuffs of your socks. Remove the head. Cut out two cloth strips from the bedsheet. Make each strip as long as the measurement, and about as wide as your own leg.

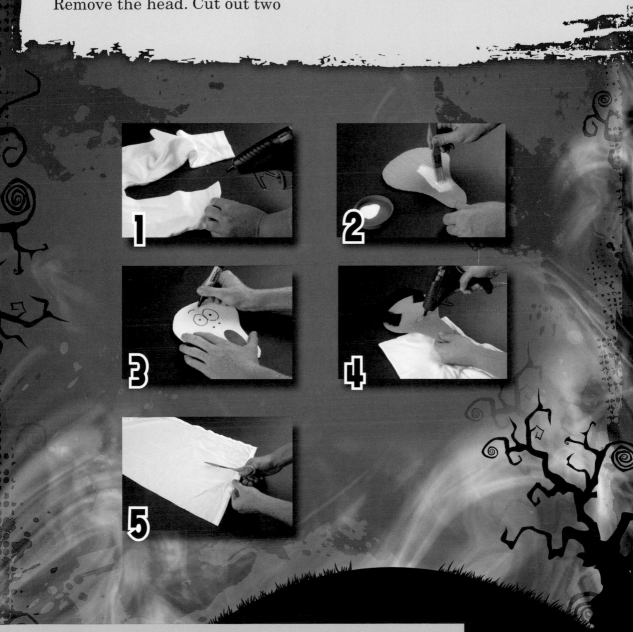

illusion—something that appears to be real but isn't

Step 6: Cut the second pizza box lid so it's as wide as the two cloth strips when lying side-by-side. Slip the lid inside the shirt. Have an adult hot glue the top edges of the cloth strips to the lid so they hang down. They should be about the same distance apart as your own legs.

Step 7: Ask an adult to help you hot glue the shirt closed along the bottom. The white "legs" will hang down.

Step 8: Tuck the shirt cuffs inside the white gloves. Ask an adult to help you hot glue one side of each cuff to the inner wrist of each glove. Make sure you don't glue the gloves closed.

Step 9: Dress in a black hoodie and black pants. Hang the cardboard head around your neck. Tuck the ends of each white cloth strip into your socks. Pull the hood over your head, and slip on the white gloves.

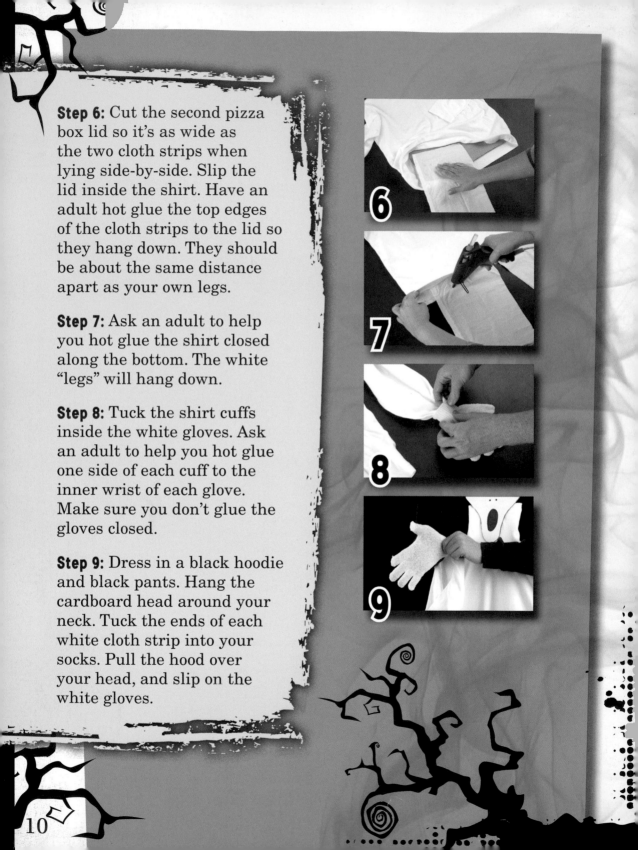

TIP: It's important to be safe while trick-or-treating. Apply reflective tape to your costume. Carry a flashlight, and always go with an adult.

Walk All Over Me

Some people dress up like movie stars for Halloween. But not many look to a movie theater for costume ideas. Let out your inner litterbug, and become the floor of a movie theater!

WHAT YOU NEED:

36-inch by 48-inch (91-cm by 122-cm) black tri-fold display board
pencil
utility scissors
red construction paper
markers
glue gun and hot glue
napkins
plastic cups
popcorn
candy boxes and candy
glasses or sunglasses
white cardstock
clear tape
red and blue cellophane
hole punch
2 medium-size, thick rubber bands

Step 1: Lie down in the middle of the display board with your arms slightly apart. Ask a friend or adult to trace your head and mark where your elbows are on the board. Cut out an oval for your face and holes for your arms.

Step 2: To make movie tickets, cut construction paper into small rectangles. Write "Admit One" on each ticket.

Step 3: Ask an adult to hot glue crumpled napkins and cups, popcorn, candy boxes, candy, and tickets to the front of the board.

Step 4: To make 3D glasses, set a pair of glasses face down on a piece of white card stock. Trace the glasses with a pencil and cut out. Then cut out the eyeholes.

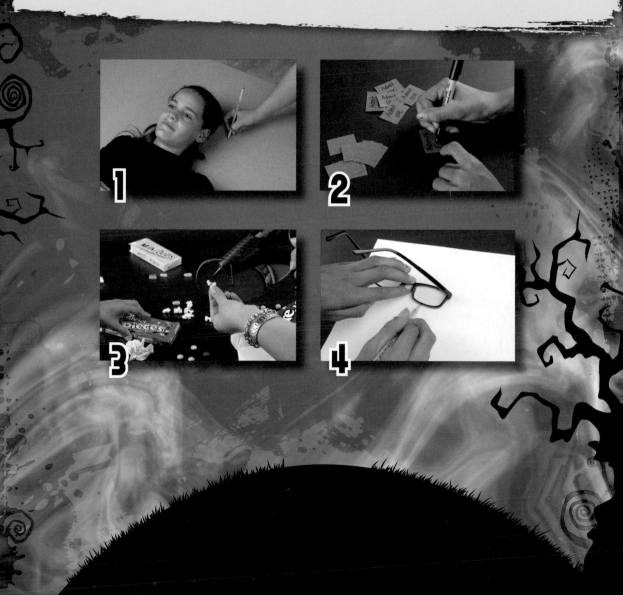

Step 5: Tape colored **cellophane** over the insides of the eyeholes.

Step 6: Punch a hole on each side of the glasses frame. Thread a rubber band through each hole. Thread one end of each rubber band through its opposite loop. This will create a knot in each rubber band. Then stretch each rubber band around your ears to hold the glasses in place.

Step 7: Slip your head and arms through the holes you cut in the board. Remove the board and carry it while walking through doorways.

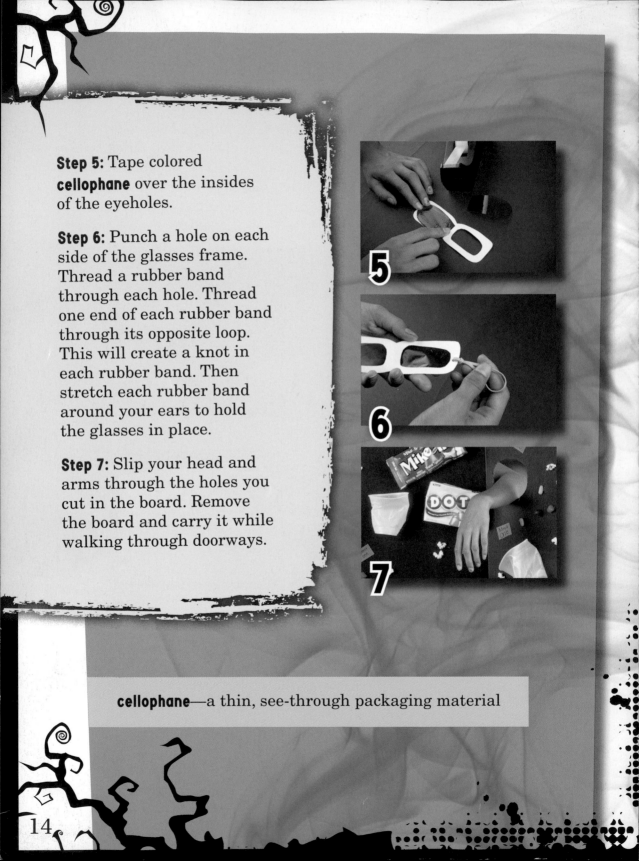

cellophane—a thin, see-through packaging material

TIP: If you're a sports fan, become the floor
of a baseball stadium! Hot glue peanut shells, hot dog buns,
and an old baseball to the cardboard. Wear a baseball cap.

Call of the Wild

You're sure to have a howling good time in this costume. Dress up as a werewolf that's been caught halfway through its gory transformation. From one side you'll look like a human. From the other way you'll look like a wolf!

WHAT YOU NEED:

utility scissors
long-sleeved shirt
pants
glue gun and hot glue
1 yard (0.9 meter) brown
  furlike fabric

black permanent marker
plastic lid
right-hand brown glove
brown sock
brown face paint
black eyebrow pencil

spirit gum and remover
  (carried in most
  costume stores)
hair gel

Step 1: Jaggedly cut off the right sleeve off a shirt just below the elbow. Jaggedly cut off the right leg of a pair of pants just below the knee.

Step 2: Ask an adult to hot glue patches of the furlike fabric to the shirtsleeve and pant leg you cut.

Step 3: Using a black permanent marker, draw 10 teardrop-shaped claws on the plastic lid. Color in the claws and cut out.

Step 4: Ask an adult to hot glue fake fur to the glove. Then hot glue the five plastic claws to the fingertips of the glove. Glue the other five claws to the tip of the sock.

Step 5 (not pictured): Use face paint to make the right half of your face and nose brown. Use an eyebrow pencil to darken your right eyebrow.

Step 6: Cut a 2-inch (5-cm) long fake fur triangle for a sideburn. Use spirit gum to attach it to your face.

Step 7: To make a wolf ear, cut a 5-inch (13-cm) long teardrop shape from the furlike fabric. Cut a slit down the center. Slip your real ear through the slit.

Step 8 (not pictured): Use hair gel to spike up your hair on the right side. Slick down your hair on the left side.

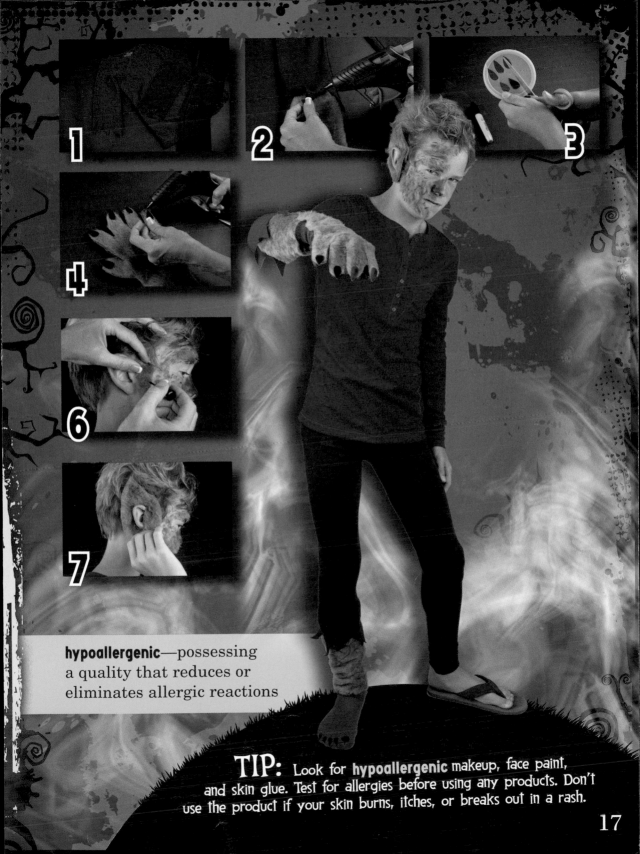

1 **2** **3**

4

6

7

hypoallergenic—possessing
a quality that reduces or
eliminates allergic reactions

TIP: Look for **hypoallergenic** makeup, face paint,
and skin glue. Test for allergies before using any products. Don't
use the product if your skin burns, itches, or breaks out in a rash.

Raggedy Ruckus

This disturbed doll is no pushover. If there's a rumble, she'll be there. Even with a dangling arm, she's still dangerous. Use cotton balls and plastic bags to become the doll that rules the toy room!

WHAT YOU NEED:

scissors
long-sleeved dress
paintbrush
red acrylic paint
white cloth gloves

plastic bags
glue gun and hot glue
cotton balls
white tights
aluminum foil

boots
white face paint
black eyebrow pencil
black lipstick
black ribbon or yarn

Step 1: Partially cut off one sleeve of the dress at the shoulder. Leave part of the sleeve connected so it dangles. Paint the edges red. Let dry.

Step 2: Stuff one glove and the dangling sleeve with plastic bags. Tuck the cuff into the glove. Ask an adult to hot glue them together. Pull apart cotton balls, and ask an adult to hot glue them to the shoulder opening.

Step 3: Cut a few slits in the tights and dress. Ask an adult to hot glue cotton balls around the slits. Splatter your outfit with red paint. Let dry.

Step 4: To create a chain necklace, cut pieces of aluminum foil into long strips. Roll up each strip lengthwise.

Twist the ends of one piece together. Then insert the second piece through the first piece, and twist the ends together. Continue until you have a long necklace.

Step 5 (not pictured): Put on the dress, tights, necklace, and boots.

Step 6 (not pictured): Use face paint to paint your face white. Blacken one eye with an eyebrow pencil. Draw eyelashes below the other eye and a black triangle on your nose. Apply black lipstick.

Step 7: Tease your hair and add a black ribbon. On the side with the dangling sleeve, tuck your arm into the dress. Put on the other glove.

tease—to comb hair by taking hold of a strand and pushing the hairs toward the scalp with the comb

TIP: Start with any "nice" costume and then rough it up. Imagine a scary Santa Claus or Spider-Man.

Operation Disaster

Your worst nightmare has come true! Are those your **intestines**? Of course they are—you made them yourself with newspaper, tape, and paint! Gross out your friends in this horrifying costume.

WHAT YOU NEED:

scissors
ruler
large shoe box
paintbrush
pink acrylic paint
newspaper
masking tape
red spray paint
white glue
heavy book
old bedsheet
glue gun and hot glue
white and black
 face paint
shower cap
salad tongs

Step 1: Cut down 2 inches (5 cm) on each corner of the shoe box. Fold back the box flaps on all four sides.

Step 2: Paint the inside of the box pink. Let dry.

Step 3: Twist and tape newspaper pages together to form a 6-foot (1.8-meter) long rope.

Step 4: Spray paint the newspaper rope red. Follow the instructions and safety precautions on the can. Let dry.

Step 5: Coat the inside bottom of the shoe box with white glue. Zigzag the paper intestines into the box. Set a heavy book on top of the intestines while the glue dries.

Step 6: Cut out two 2- by 48-inch (5- by 122-cm) strips from the bedsheet and set aside. Spread the rest of the sheet on the floor.

Ask an adult to put hot glue on the flaps of the box. Flip the box face down on the center of the sheet to secure. Let dry.

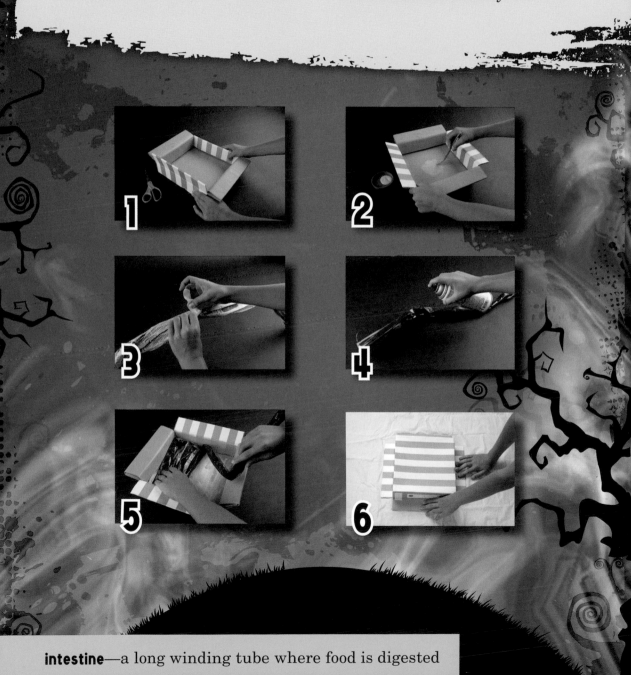

intestine—a long winding tube where food is digested

Step 7: Center the two cloth strips across top and bottom edges on the back of the box. Ask an adult to hot glue the cloth strips in place.

Step 8: Flip the sheet and the box over. Cut a square in the sheet to show the intestines.

Step 9: Using face paint, make your face white. Add black shadows under your eyes. Tuck your hair into the shower cap.

Step 10: Have an adult tie the box around your stomach and the sheet around your torso. Pull the top corners of the sheet under your arms and tie in a double knot behind you. If needed, trim the bottom edge of the sheet so you won't trip. Carry the salad tongs.

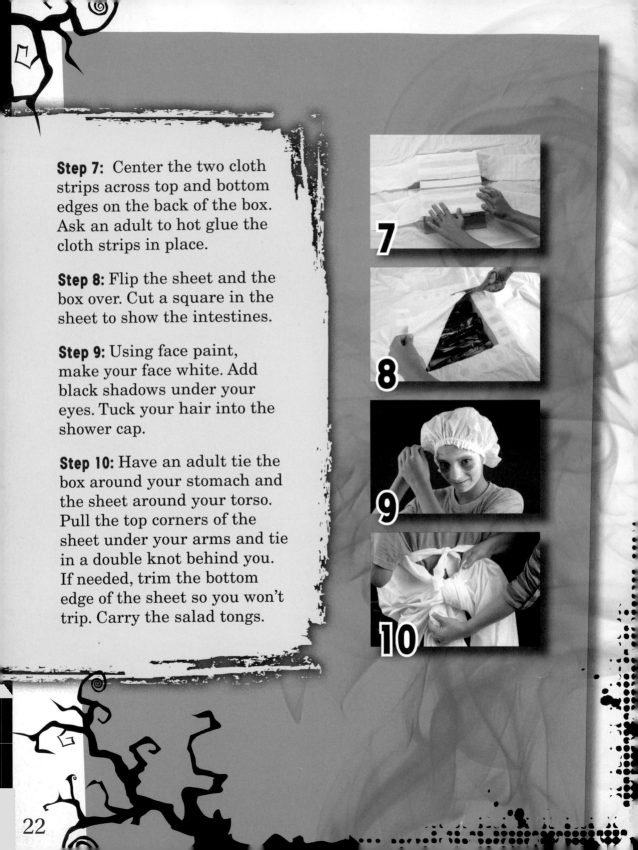

flame-retardant—made
or treated so as to
resist burning

TIP: Always keep your costume away
from open flames when trick-or-treating.
You should also make sure your costume is
flame-retardant. Have an adult spray your costume
with a flame-retardant solution. Then let the costume dry.

23

Fanged Rocker

Anyone can throw on a black cape and some fangs to be a vampire for Halloween. Why not change things up and become a rocker vampire that's been staked with his own guitar?

WHAT YOU NEED:

pencil
large piece of cardboard
utility scissors
cardboard wrapping
   paper tube
ruler
glue gun and hot glue
paintbrush
acrylic paints
old bedsheet, cut into
   a 2- by 48-inch
   (5- by 122-cm) strip
black shirt
face paint
black eyebrow pencil
plastic fangs
vampire cape

Step 1: Draw the body of a guitar on a large piece of cardboard. Cut out with the utility scissors.

Step 2: Using your hands, flatten a cardboard wrapping paper tube to make the neck. Cut a 3- by 4-inch (8- by 10-cm) cardboard rectangle to make the head. Ask an adult to help you hot glue the head to one end of the neck. Then hot glue the other end of the neck to the guitar body.

Step 3: Paint the head, neck, and guitar body. Let dry. Paint white lines across the neck. Paint six white dots on the edges of the head. Let dry.

Step 4: Cut the neck in half at an angle. Fringe the end of neck that isn't attached to the guitar body. Fold back the tabs. Have an adult hot glue the tabs to a 4- by 4-inch (10- by 10-cm) scrap of cardboard. Center the cardboard square on the cloth strip. Then glue the cloth strip to the back of the cardboard.

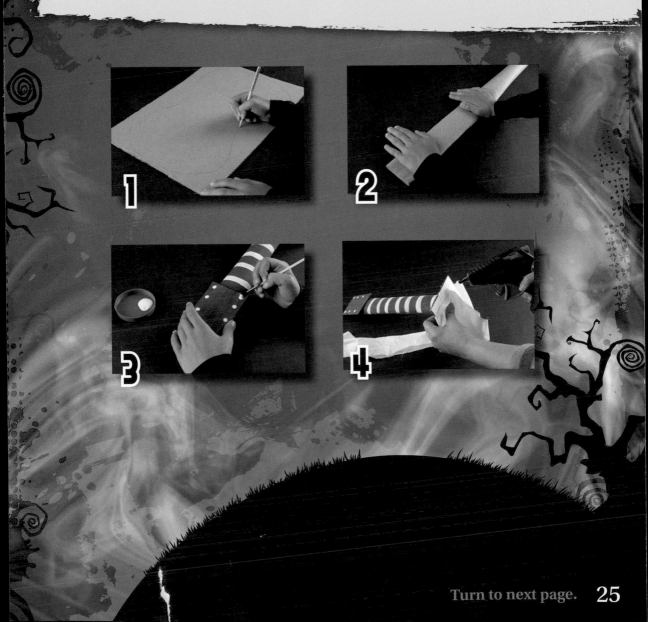

Turn to next page.

Step 5: Cut a slit in your shirt where the head and neck of the guitar will stick out. Paint red around the slit. Drip red down the front of the shirt. Let dry.

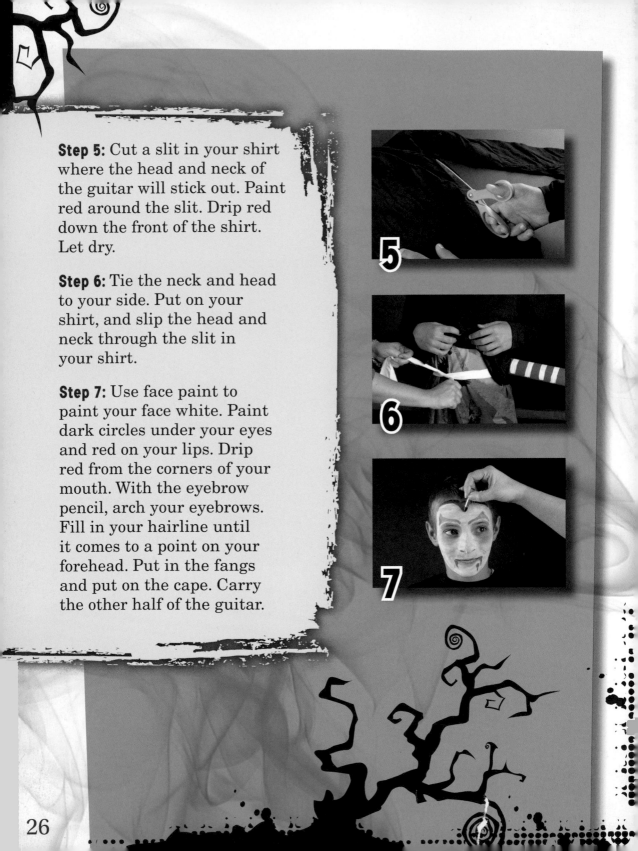

Step 6: Tie the neck and head to your side. Put on your shirt, and slip the head and neck through the slit in your shirt.

Step 7: Use face paint to paint your face white. Paint dark circles under your eyes and red on your lips. Drip red from the corners of your mouth. With the eyebrow pencil, arch your eyebrows. Fill in your hairline until it comes to a point on your forehead. Put in the fangs and put on the cape. Carry the other half of the guitar.

TIP: Create a vampire rock band with your friends. Stake one friend with a microphone and another with a drumstick. Create the microphone from the cardboard wrapping tube. Wrap it in aluminum foil and use a black foam ball for the tip. Use brown construction paper and masking tape to make the drumstick.

Good Enough to Eat

Caught in the spider's web, there's no way to escape! This hairy monster holds your head in a death grip. Comfort yourself by knowing her **spiderlings** will be well fed.

WHAT YOU NEED:

white marker
9- by 11-inch (23- by
 28-cm) piece of black felt
ruler
scissors
glue gun and hot glue

newspaper
white and red
 craft foam
8 1- by 30-inch (2.5- by
 76-cm) strips of
 black fabric

black chenille stems
large black pom-poms
white long-sleeved shirt
white sheet
tulle

spiderling—a young spider

Step 1 (not pictured): Using the white marker, draw two 4-inch (10-cm) circles and two 6-inch (15-cm) circles on black felt. Cut out with scissors.

Step 2 (not pictured): Match up the large and small circles. Ask an adult to help you hot glue the edges of the matched circles together. Leave an opening on each circle. Let dry.

Step 3: Stuff the circles with newspaper. Ask an adult to hot glue them closed.

Step 4: Cut out eyes and fangs from white foam. Ask an adult to hot glue them to the smaller circle. Cut pupils from the red foam and ask an adult to hot glue them to the eyes. Glue the spider's head to its body.

Step 5: To make the spider's legs, ask an adult to help you hot glue eight black cloth strips to the underside of the spider's body.

Step 6: To make a spiderling, twist four chenille stems together. Spread the legs apart. Have an adult hot glue the legs to the center of a large black pom-pom. Repeat for as many spiderlings as you'd like to make.

Step 7: Put on the white shirt. Stand with your arms away from your body. Have an adult wrap the white sheet around your torso. Leave holes for your arms. Tie the ends of the sheet to each other. Wrap tulle around the sheet. Hook the spiderlings' legs into the tulle to hold them in place.

Step 8: Tie the felt spider to your head with its legs. Position the spider so it covers one of your eyes.

Lift the spider off of your eye as you walk so you can see where you're going.

TIP: What other bugs might get caught in the spider's web? Twist together different colored pipe cleaners to make worms, caterpillars, flies, and other kinds of creepy creatures.

Glossary

cellophane (SEL-uh-fayn)—a thin, clear material made from cellulose, used to wrap food and to make clear tape

flame-retardant (FLAYM-ri-TARD-uhnt)—made or treated so as to resist burning

hypoallergenic (hye-poh-a-luhr-JEN-ik)—possessing a quality that reduces or eliminates allergic reactions

illusion (i-LOO-zhuhn)—something that appears to be real but isn't

intestine (in-TES-tin)—a long winding tube where food is digested; humans have a large and small intestine

spiderling (SPYE-dur-ling)—a young spider

tease (TEEZ)—to comb hair by taking hold of a strand and pushing the hairs toward the scalp with a comb

Read More

Brown, Tessa. *Costume Crafts*. Creative Crafts for Kids. New York: Gareth Stevens Pub., 2010.

Ipcizade, Catherine. *How to Make Frightening Halloween Decorations*. Halloween Extreme. Mankato, Minn.: Capstone Press, 2011.

McGee, Randel. *Paper Crafts for Halloween*. Paper Craft Fun for Holidays. Berkeley Heights, N.J., Enslow Elementary, 2009.

Skillicorn, Helen. *Spooky Crafts*. Creative Crafts for Kids. New York: Gareth Stevens Pub., 2010.

Internet Sites

FactHound offers a safe, fun way to find Internet sites related to this book. All of the sites on FactHound have been researched by our staff.

Here's all you do:

Visit *www.facthound.com*

Type in this code: 9781429654227

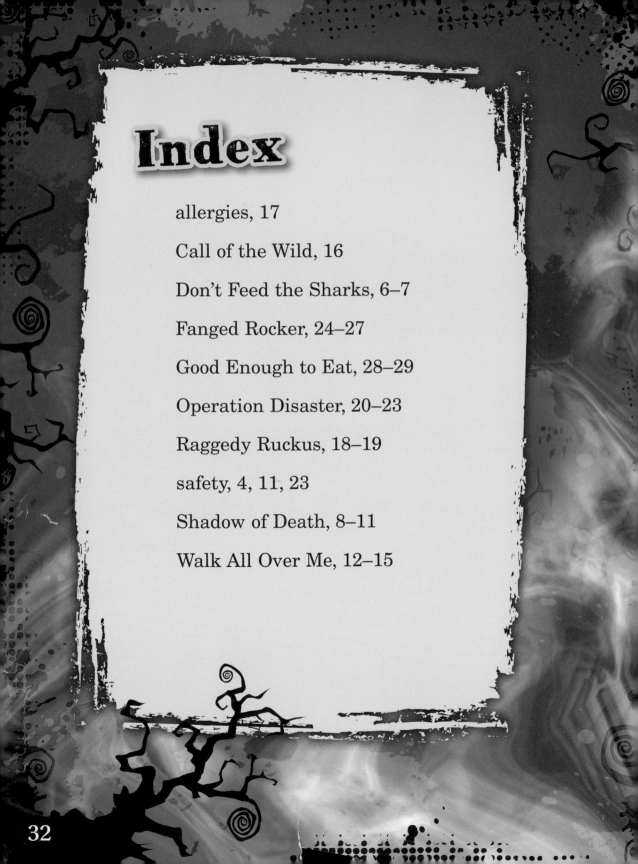

Index